ANIMAL
SUPERSTARS

CHIMPANZEE
BRAINY BEAST

PAIGE V. POLINSKY

CONSULTING EDITOR, DIANE CRAIG, M.A./READING SPECIALIST

Super Sandcastle

An Imprint of Abdo Publishing
abdopublishing.com

abdopublishing.com

Published by Abdo Publishing, a division of ABDO, PO Box 398166, Minneapolis, Minnesota 55439. Copyright © 2017 by Abdo Consulting Group, Inc. International copyrights reserved in all countries. No part of this book may be reproduced in any form without written permission from the publisher. Super SandCastle™ is a trademark and logo of Abdo Publishing.

Printed in the United States of America, North Mankato, Minnesota
062016
092016

THIS BOOK CONTAINS
RECYCLED MATERIALS

Editor: Rebecca Felix
Content Developer: Nancy Tuminelly
Cover and Interior Design and Production: Christa Schneider, Mighty Media, Inc.
Photo Credits: iStockphoto; Mighty Media, Inc.; Shutterstock

Library of Congress Cataloging-in-Publication Data

Names: Polinsky, Paige V., author.
Title: Chimpanzee : brainy beast / by Paige V. Polinsky.
Description: Minneapolis, Minnesota : Abdo Publishing, [2017] | Series:
    Animal superstars
Identifiers: LCCN 2016006312 (print) | LCCN 2016007037 (ebook) | ISBN
    9781680781472 (print) | ISBN 9781680775907 (ebook)
Subjects: LCSH: Chimpanzees--Juvenile literature.
Classification: LCC QL737.P96 P655 2016 (print) | LCC QL737.P96 (ebook) | DDC
    599.885--dc23
LC record available at http://lccn.loc.gov/2016006312

Super SandCastle™ books are created by a team of professional educators, reading specialists, and content developers around five essential components—phonemic awareness, phonics, vocabulary, text comprehension, and fluency—to assist young readers as they develop reading skills and strategies and increase their general knowledge. All books are written, reviewed, and leveled for guided reading, early reading intervention, and Accelerated Reader™ programs for use in shared, guided, and independent reading and writing activities to support a balanced approach to literacy instruction.

CONTENTS

GREAT APES

Chimpanzees are in the great **ape** family. They are also our closest animal relatives! Chimps can be more than 5 feet (1.5 m) tall. They can weigh up to 130 pounds (59 kg).

5 FEET 5 INCHES (1.7 M)

AN ADULT CHIMPANZEE IS AS TALL AS AN AVERAGE ADULT WOMAN.

WAYS TO WALK

CHIMPS USUALLY WALK ON ALL FOURS.
BUT THEY CAN ALSO WALK UPRIGHT.

HANDY DIGITS

Chimps have long arms. They have short legs. They also have **opposable** thumbs. This helps chimps grab objects.

SMART TOOLS

Chimps are super smart. They make their own tools. They use stones as hammers. They use sticks to dig up insects.

TOOL KITS

SOME CHIMPS CREATE TOOL KITS. THEY COLLECT STONES, STICKS, AND MORE. THEY USE THE KITS TO GATHER CERTAIN FOODS.

TREETOP LIVING

Wild chimps live in Africa. They spend a lot of time in the trees. This is where they eat and sleep.

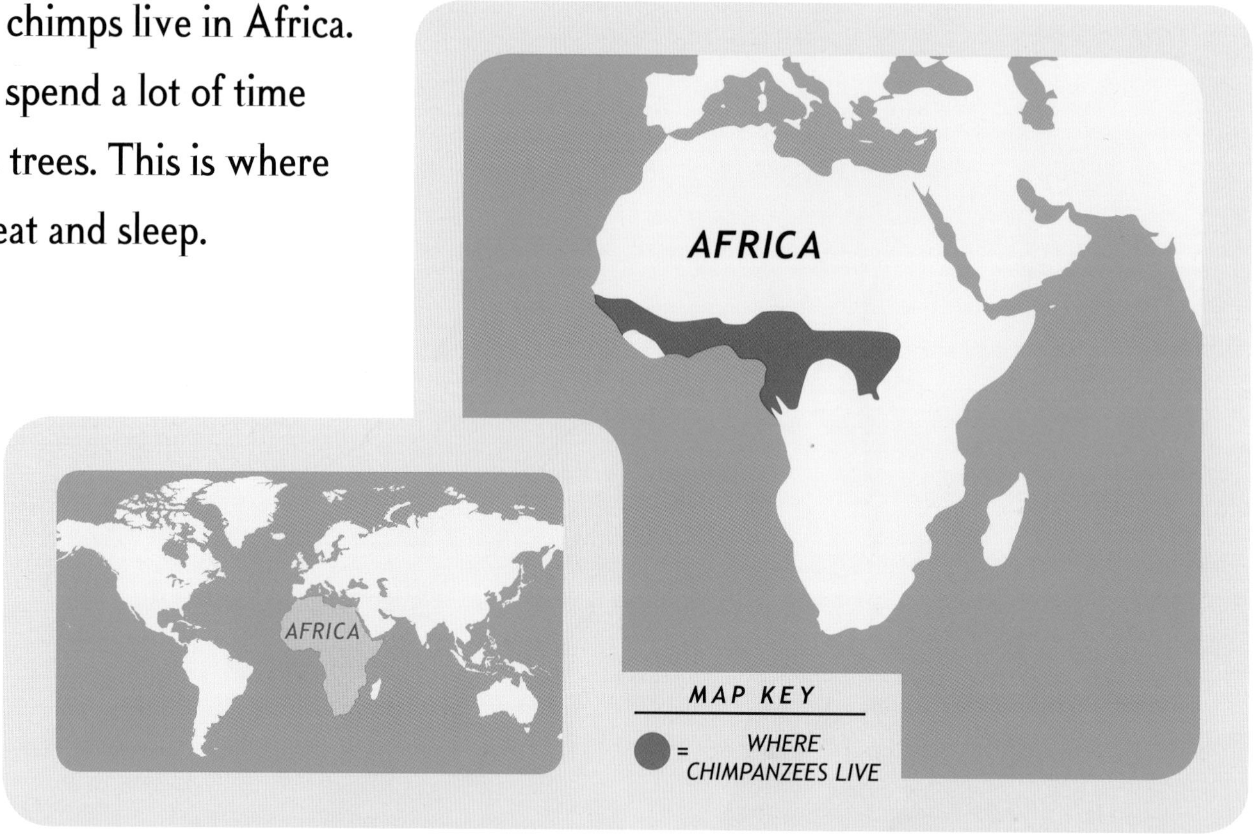

AFRICA

AFRICA

MAP KEY

● = WHERE CHIMPANZEES LIVE

Chimps do not live alone. They form communities.

GREAT GROUPS

Chimps in a community work together. They search for food. They also fight **intruders**. Male chimps compete to become leader. And most chimps create friend groups. Friends play with and **groom** each other.

CHATTY CHIMPS

Chimps communicate in many ways. They use sounds. They also use **gestures**. Chimps laugh and even kiss!

Chimps can also communicate with humans. People have taught **sign language** to some chimps.

SNACK SKILLS

Chimpanzees eat fruit, insects, and more. It takes a strong memory to know where to find each food. Sometimes chimps hunt other animals together. They use wooden spears.

BABY BONDS

Mother chimps raise their young for years. Their bond is strong. Female chimps often help each other with this care. Males act as fathers to all young chimps.

FOREVER FAMILY

ORPHAN CHIMPS ARE OFTEN RAISED BY SIBLINGS. SOMETIMES UNRELATED CHIMPS RAISE THE ORPHANS.

APES IN DANGER

People hunt chimpanzees. They sell their meat. They also sell chimps as pets. Today, chimps are **endangered**. But many people work to protect the world's remaining chimps.

CHIMPANZEE SUPERSTAR

Can you imagine a chimpanzee superstar? What **awards** would it win?

WHAT DO YOU KNOW ABOUT
CHIMPANZEES?

1. Chimps have short arms and long legs.

True or false?

2. Chimps use tools to gather food.

True or false?

3. Chimps often live by themselves.

True or false?

4. Chimps can learn **sign language.**

True or false?

ANSWERS:
1. FALSE 2. TRUE 3. FALSE 4. TRUE

GLOSSARY

APE - a large animal related to humans and monkeys. Chimpanzees and gorillas are apes.

AWARD - a prize.

ENDANGERED - having few of a type of plant or animal left in the world.

GESTURE - a motion made to express meaning.

GROOM - to clean oneself and take care of one's appearance.

INTRUDER - a being that goes somewhere it is not welcome.

OPPOSABLE - able to be placed against other digits of a hand or foot to grip things.

ORPHAN - a being who doesn't have any parents.

SIGN LANGUAGE - a language in which gestures are used instead of speech.